sensory deprivation

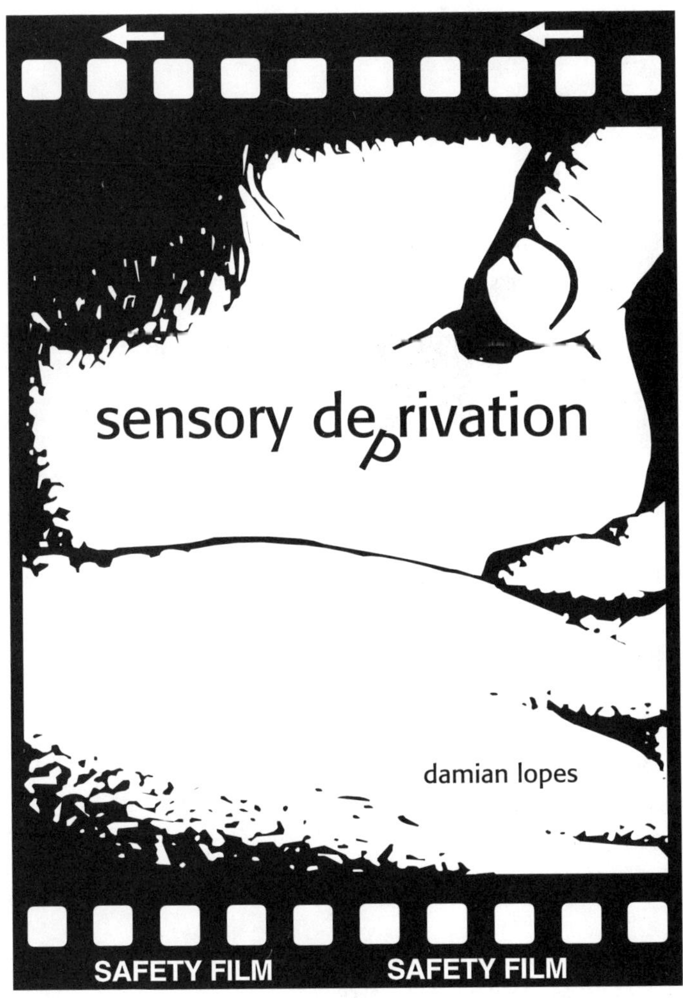

Coach House Books

first edition

Published with the assistance of the Canada Council for the Arts and the Ontario Arts Council.

CANADIAN CATALOGUING IN PUBLICATION DATA

Lopes, Damian
Sensory deprivation

Poems.
ISBN 1-55245-052-X (boxed)
ISBN 1-55245-020-1 (pbk)

I. Title

PS8573.O637S46 2000 C811'.54 C99-930125-X
PR9199.3.L66S46 2000

for Dom

socratic prophecies: an introduction

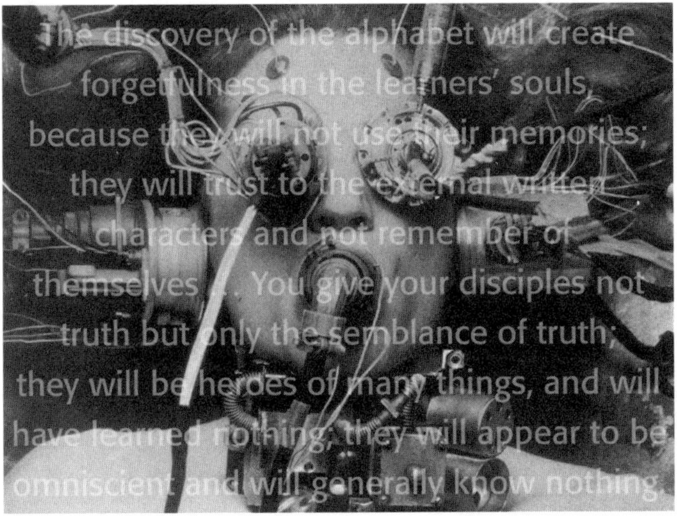

The discovery of the alphabet will create forgetfulness in the learners' souls, because they will not use their memories; they will trust to the external written characters and not remember of themselves . . . You give your disciples not truth but only the semblance of truth; they will be heroes of many things, and will have learned nothing; they will appear to be omniscient and will generally know nothing.

Fig 17-3. Linguistic metabolizer

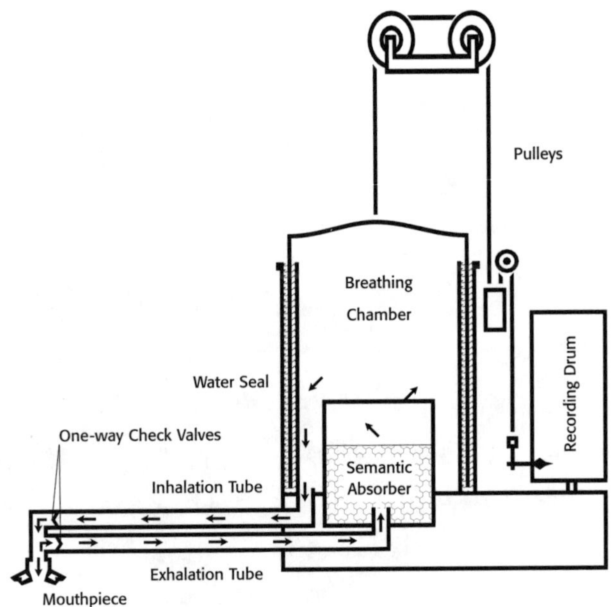

Apparatus designed to metabolize vocal utterances and codify them visually on a recording drum. The absorbefacient (any commoditized medium) is consumed at a rate directly proportionate to the square of the metaphoric content.

gramma berida
glandri galassassa laul-
beri bin blassa glassala
sassala bim
zimzalla binban
bin beri ban o
ossola hop-
o gadjama
bluku

the avant-garde in memoriam

tristan tzara reads in zurich, 1916

buying Tickle-Me-Elmo, 1996

the man you script

.watching .waiting & watching .silent .voyeur .voir .an act .a window .seeing .a part of .apart from .outside .being .separate .see pirate .unseen .evasion

.invasion .from which you derive pleasure .a sure pleaser .history .any story but your story .like tv .a transmitted visual dis-ease .flickering lights .eyes .flick flick .flick flick .sleeping eyes awake .seeing .unseen .flic .qui voit .an unspoken law .wall

.third person masculine singular .history .impersonal .or in person .high art .or a tall tale

a voice in a nondescript place & time listening to a
disembodied voice breath without body without organ
without origin a voice with a script a nondescript not a
void but a voice in a time & place watching & finding a
voice that speaks but cannot hear a cul-de-sac echoes

sound (sensation caused by vibration of surrounding air
what is or maybe heard   vibrations whether audible or
not) formed in larynx & uttered by mouth

i a letter from a word   taken out of context

(tired of weighing the prose & contexts   subverting the convention   the other of necessity   conceived after shaking off the con doomed fallacy of the con questing for the troll hiding in the blankness the words become in con sequential a series of letters a train of cons too true tempting temporary descension)

the i of the id of the entity   the eye of the story   high storey buildings   ramadan in jericho let's begin with it . like any other . written . to survive . live on top of . in writing . transformed . like every other . it becomes a fiction . existing . nonexistent . in the moment of writing . a fiction . if it never is . or was . it might remain . the moment it is . thought . written . therefore a fiction . hereto a fiction . it can be . if it remains . unknown .

every mark . a friction .

the narrator: the voice of the text. the author creates the voice but it may have a will of its own. the author believes control is complete but the author is wrong. it is quite common. they do not admit it.

authority: an itty bit of author. they like & seek power. divine creation. they want to manipulate those they cannot because they do not listen. authors are inadequate. many are beautiful losers but beautiful losers lose as well.

a narrator is to an author what man is to god & what god is to man: a failed fiction. the narrator's existence is limited. vengeance is mine writes the author.

i wrote a poem for you   hazel eyes
burning suns
melting the world
melding our souls

i wrote a poem for you   ice-blue eyes
what they wouldn't tell
freezing
never melting

i wrote a poem for you   amber eyes
make me
queasy
butterfleyes

i wrote a poem for you   one glance
destroyed you

nonvel: a summary

the narrator who is called the author is a character in this story which he says he is writing. he writes to another character who is called the reader but is not the reader although she reads what the narrator writes for her.

the narrator is not the author.

the narrator writes a story with a narrator who writes a story about a narrator writing a story for another character to another character who is affectionately referred to as the reader.

all stories are coincidental. any resemblance is fictional.

i was developing an idea for an open ended poem that
would use the stretch of street that i can see from my
window as an open ended vehicle that would allow for
the ideal shifting back & forth rather than snaring circular
movement to keep the poem from getting trapped in any
constricting pattern other than the street metaphor itself
which would work as a consistent force ensuring that the
entire project would not slip into that abyss of banal
triteness that threatens all great work

the idea was aborted on the first day of observation when
a flatbed truck drove under my window carrying a hearse

unnovel: a play

many say she's the anti-hero because they think she doesn't have what it takes to be a hero. she's definitely not a heroine.

as the story unfolds, an improbably polite pilot becomes inexorably entangled in the plot as a result of his name. but all he really does is say up yours is a matter of perspective.

the plot is a small slab of concrete in the backyard of a tenement, seen through heavily curtained windows.

many think their lives are incomplete stories . in complete stories . please complete . delete . delete . delete . delete .

sentenced to death . most don't even live once .

reading a rite of writing that tries to right . an act of decomposition . unwriting . apt loss at the end . a bow .

life personified by a bottle . mortifying isn't it .

thrust . no words of my own .

with every word   a restriction
so many possibilities opened
so many   options   closed
                    openclose

every word implies the absence of every other word
nothing implies thing   two poets speak

what is thought is what is written is different from what is
thought is what is written is different from what is read is
impossible to write

in between their lies the truth of what is just
in between words there lies what is said
in between voice & ear they're lies

silence
enough to continue

requiem for the avant-garde

twelve white men in ordered succession stand in an idle pub to regurgitate carefully rehearsed dada protest commodity. primal screams of ignoble savages in neutral zurich defying the brutality of a world gone mad with african rhythms imagined over pints of beer, around the body counts of colonial armies. this is not increased insistence of anti-art carefully documented & preserved but screams of men out of power fetishizing images of grandeur & freedom on darker backs in this wreckroom of the avant-mort. a corpus exhumed without thought as offering.

in accordance with its definition the story is never as it is supposed to be. all accurate definitions are unknown: reality displaces actuality. the story is inaccurate inconsistent & nonexistent. the story is of no interest.

the plot is just that & a way of conveying. there is no metaphor no symbolism no allegory. the truth of the matter is not found here.

this is a plot but not the one suspected & a story without meaning that is part of every story. meaning is what is not said.

stories are not to be told. they are telling. simply it is difficult. & who's to tell when the story's been told.

Fig 17-6. Inspiration calorimeter

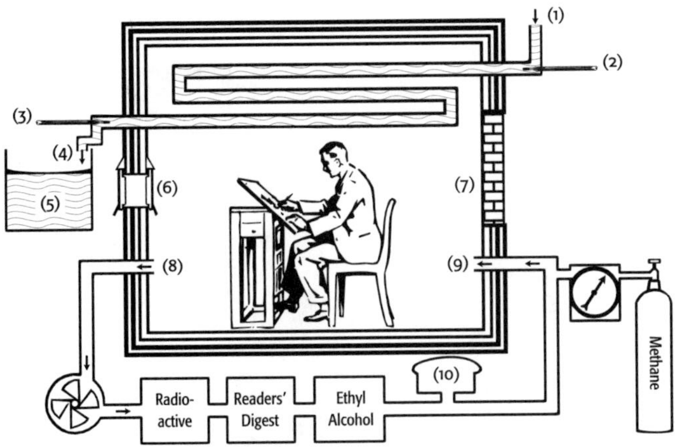

Influence flows from (1) to (4), and its temperature is measured at the inlet and outlet. Experience leaves at (8); cultural inheritance is absorbed by radioactive popular culture, originality is neutralized by Readers' Digest, residual theistic traits are denatured by ethyl alcohol, and heated flatulence is added at a measured rate; the gas mixture re-enters the chamber at (9).(2), inlet thermometer; (3), outlet thermometer; (5), see Fig 17-7; (6), sealed porthole; (7), brick window; (10), metaphoric cushion.

Fig 17-7 Influential detail

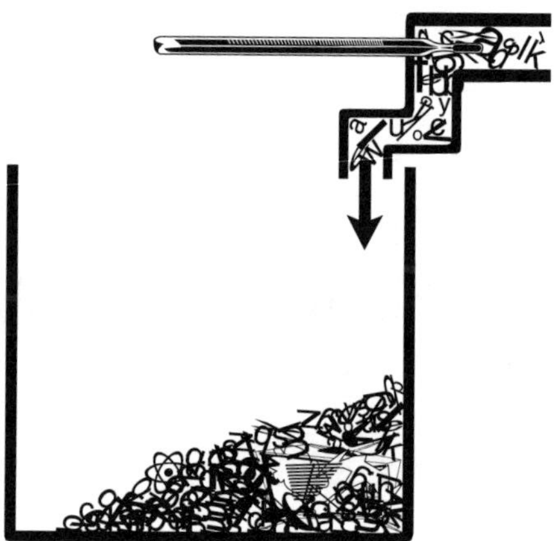

The Gutenblur
The interiorization of the technology of
the phonetic alphabet translates man from the
magical world of the ear to the neutral visual
world... Media such as letters alter the ratio
among our senses and change mental proc-
esses. When technology extends one of our
senses, a new translation of culture occurs as
swiftly as the new technology is interiorized.
The interiorization of the technology of the
phonetic alphabet translates man from the magical
world of the ear to the neutral visual world...
Media alter the ratio among our senses and
change mental processes. When technology extends
one of our senses, a new translation of culture occurs
as swiftly as the new technology is interiorized.
SAFETY FILM
SAFETY FILM
SAFETY FILM
SAFETY FILM

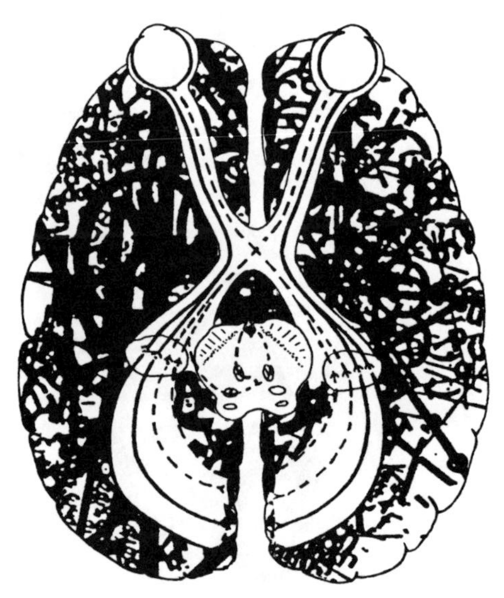

UNDERWOOD

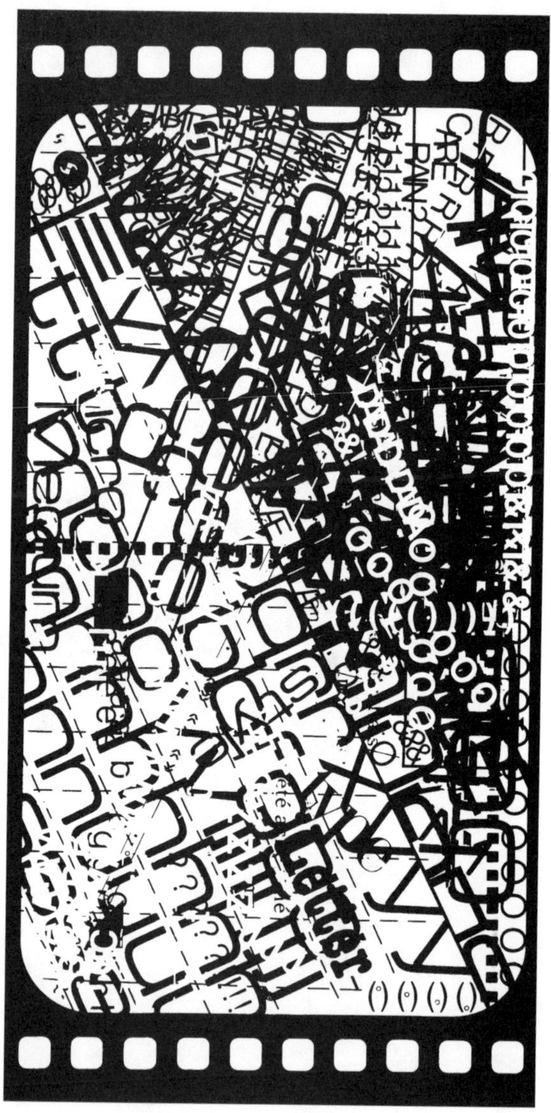

translation

after Marshall McLuhan

uno vèrso

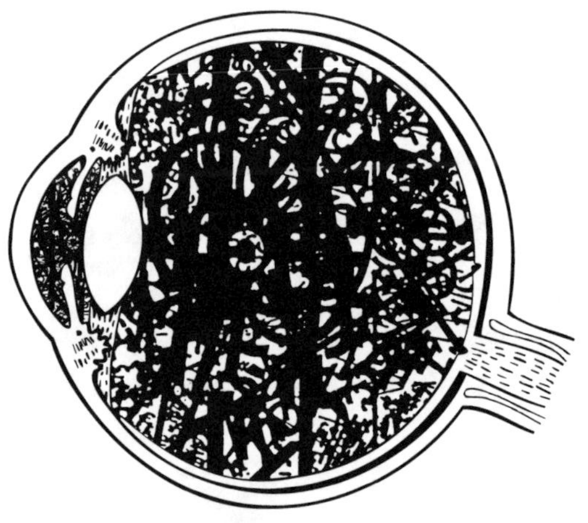

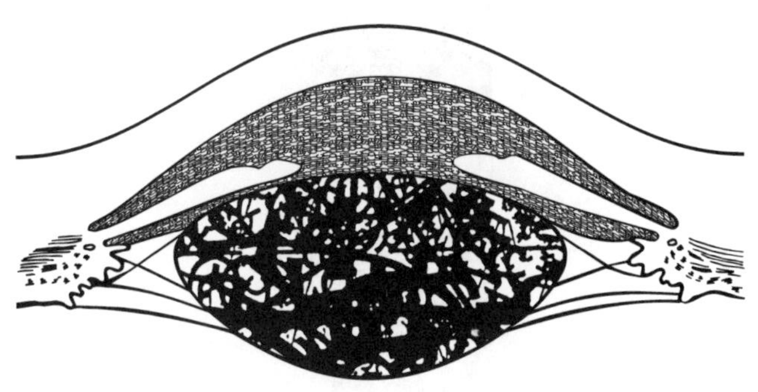

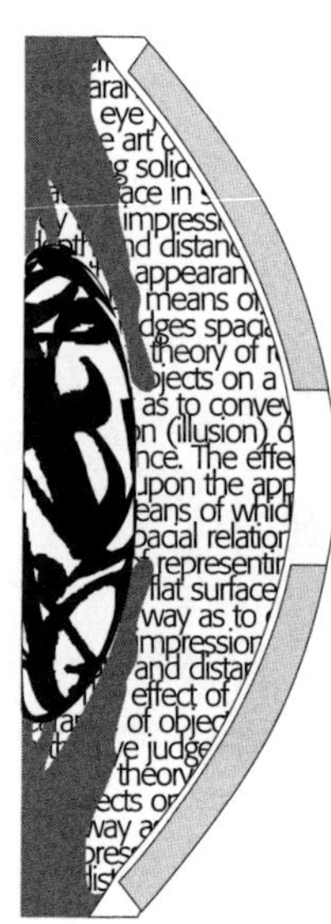

eye
e art o
g solid
ace in s
impressi
nd distanc
appearan
means of
dges spacia
theory of r
bjects on a
as to convey
n (illusion) o
nce. The effe
upon the app
eans of which
pacial relation
representin
flat surface
way as to
mpression
and distan
effect of
of objec
e judge
theory
ects or
way a
pres
list

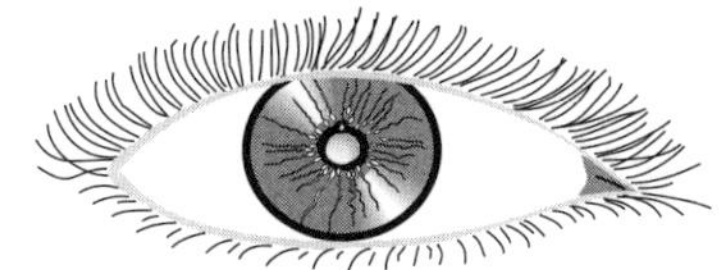

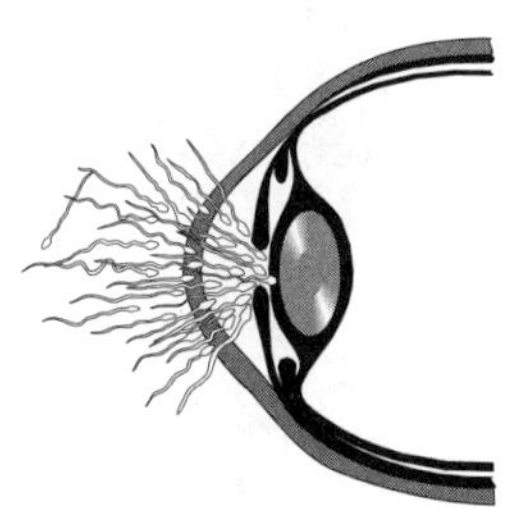

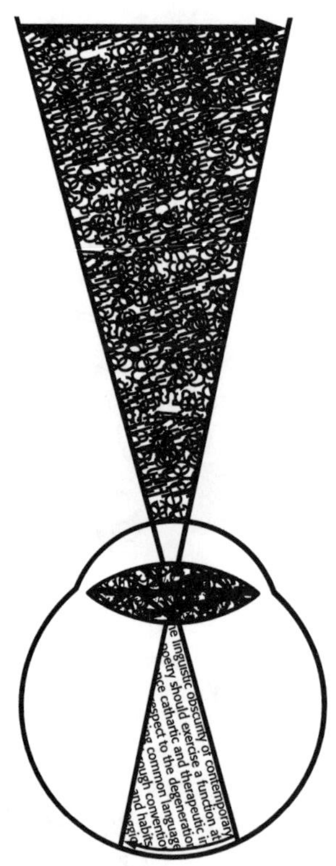
linguistic obscurity of contemporary
poetry should exercise a function at
cathartic and therapeutic in
espect to the degeneration
common language
conventio
and habits

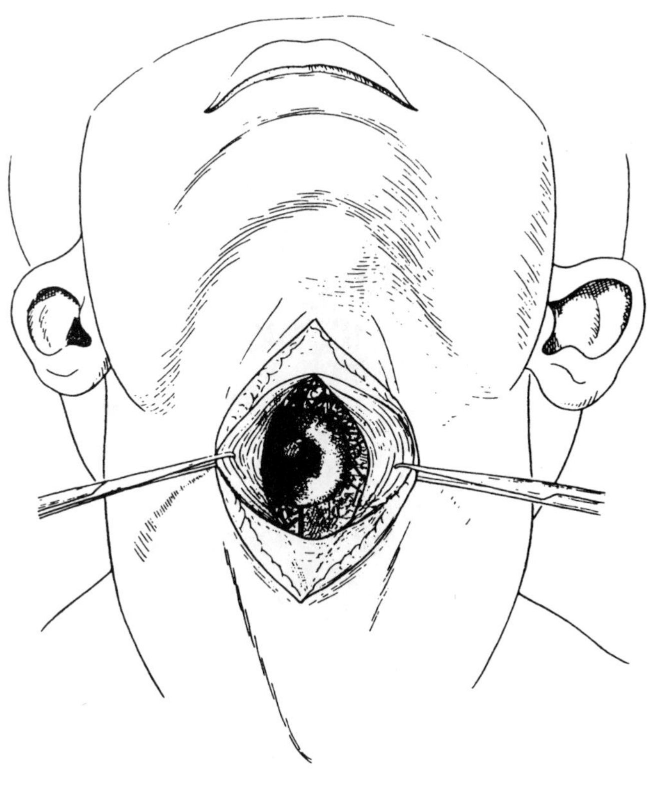

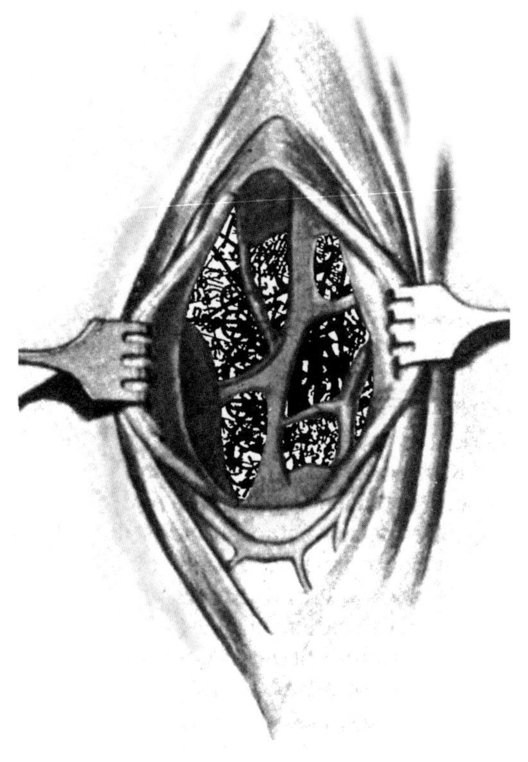

hoarse sense

for David UU

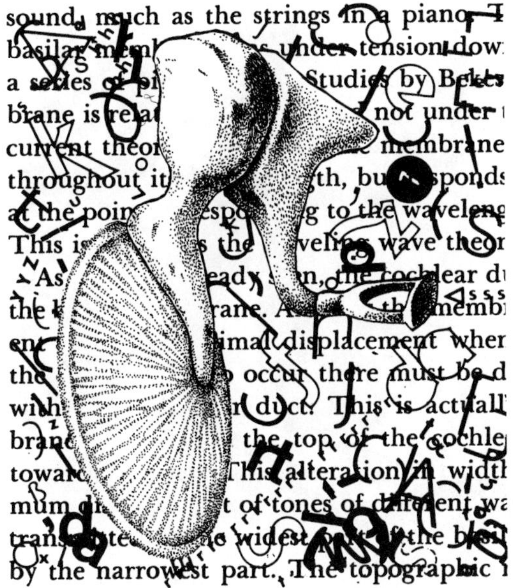

AUTO MIRANDA EC 1:1.8 f=50 mm
49ø LENS MADE IN JAPAN 2081524
RE·II
MIRANDA

YES, THAT'S RIGHT—*LOOK* AT *HIM*
HALF-*THING!* *MAN* IS MORE AT HOME WITH UNSPEAKING *MACHINES* THAN IN THE COMPANY OF MORTAL CREATURES!

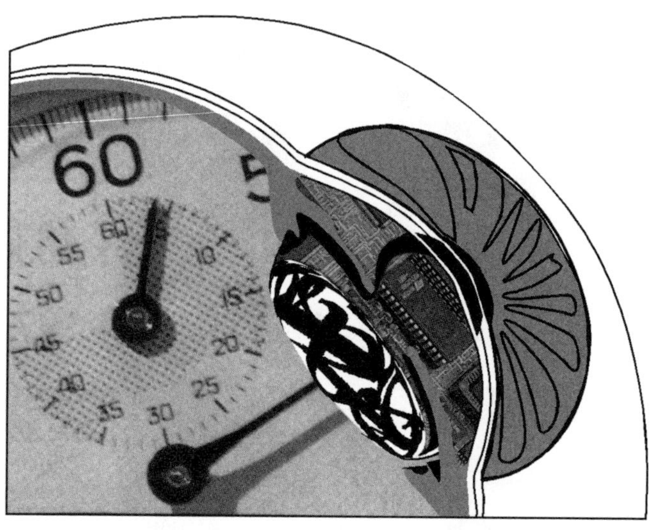
60
60
10
15
20
25
30
35
40
45
50
55

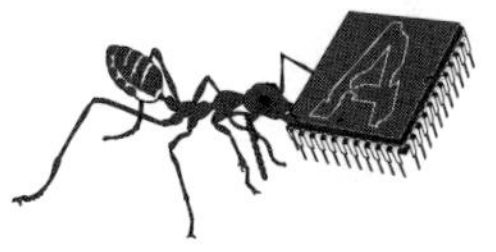

do not readjust your set
do not readjust your set
do not justread your set

a found calendar

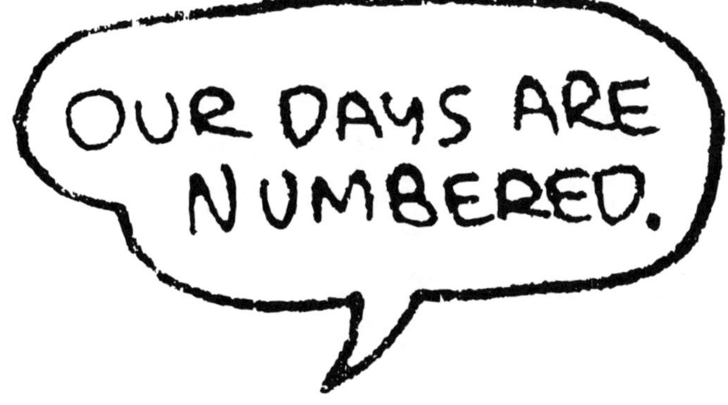

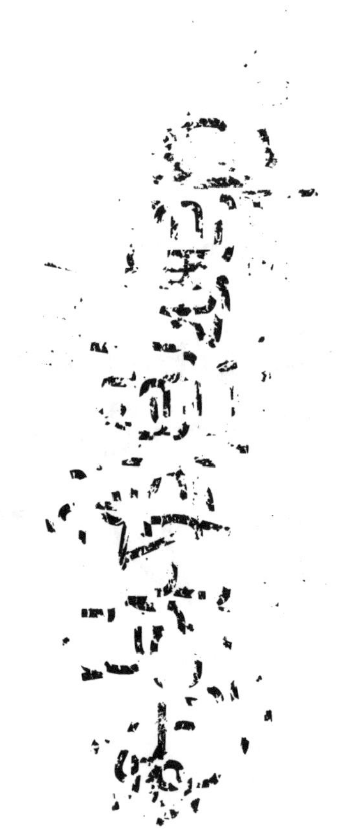

initial

stand on guard

after Ashis Nandy

Thus, what looks like obfuscation and compromise with evil may be seen also as a truer understanding of the oppressors whose suffering and decadence is, for once, taken seriously by their victims, who bear the responsibility of being both the subject and the object of 'history'. What looks like a failure to make cognitive distinctions may in fact be a recognition that the popular modern antonyms are not always the true opposites. This century has shown that in every situation of organized oppression the true antonyms are always the exclusive part versus the inclusive whole – not masculinity versus femininity but either of them versus androgyny, not past versus the present but either of them versus the timelessness in which the past is the present and the present is the past, not the oppressor versus the oppressed but both of them versus the rationality which turns them into co-victims.

ive got the oar
ive got the oa
ive got the o
ive got the

continuum

ive got th
ive got t
ive got
ive go
ive g
ive
iv
i

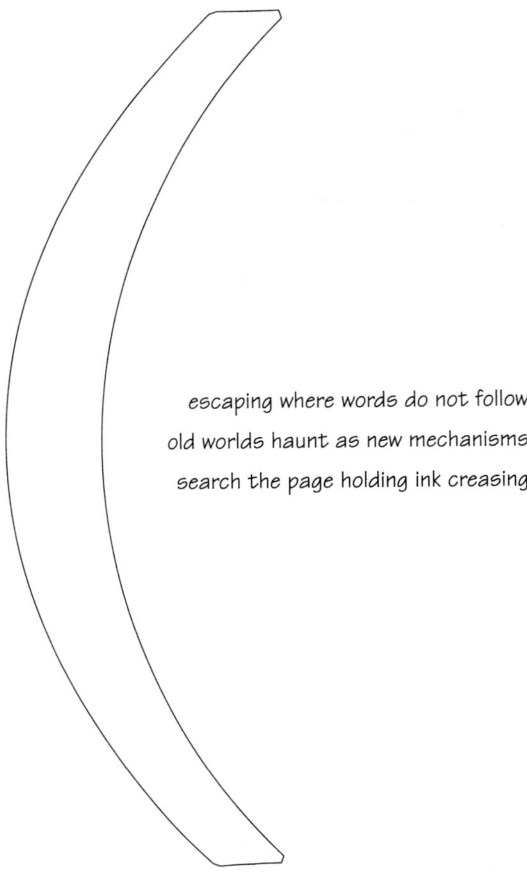

escaping where words do not follow
old worlds haunt as new mechanisms
search the page holding ink creasing

k/h

silence

moving
body
revolting

of a girl on the bus
up
stomach
twists
down
swirls
under bridges
& over

a poem written

mantra forgotten

distance
dying stance
of words
stamped into
mined heart souled

MCI
PCL
windows turn
the world green
golf course
cinder blocks
bible theme park

hydro towers like trees
underwater
tunnel
intestine

a journey from
of the hand

in silence
insistence

scratch the words
that form beneath
the hand
twist
the smudge
of ink
a reminder
in a reclusive world
of destitution

the warmth
of your breath

×   ×   ×   ↓   ↓

veins & arteries
as tide turns
to backwash
whitecaps

telephone poles sprout
young corn

6732 returns
6723 islandbound

the poem's moment
ॐ
meditation of the page

passing through the medium

the poem
personal
too one person
my i forming
this landscape
for you
the Δ elsewhere
order unknown

no one tells
the place static
aphasia of time
to bite the tongue
bleeds off the page
again the silence
until a hand

study the model
movement of form
as distance remains
past
on/off

tide out & out & out & out & out &

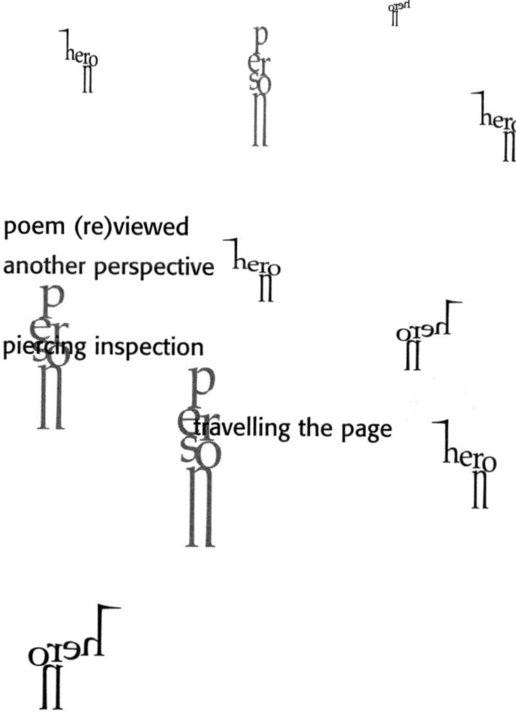

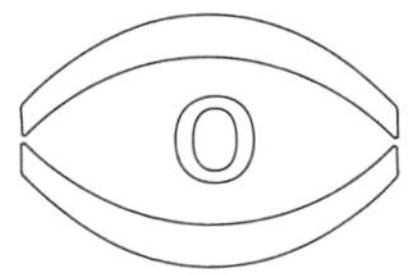

3:00

Berth 3
Deck c3

poem
self
water

birthed
at sea

3:03

a ferry comes to dock

a maze of siding
metal ramps
pulleys & wire

machines form
words letters of
integrated circuit
fluid state

Coquitlam following Burnaby

meaning seeps
sulphuric acid
memory

&

under(word)
shades

passing

counting point to light
but even the blending
can't bring the venture
curves that simulate shadows
of three dimensionality
renewal remaining
unrealized in the mind
your imagination
the only ghost

threee blasts

begin to move back
wards on
life preservers
under metal
                    bludgeons

five blasts

                    for
words unnamed
        unarmed

a small boat
                    speeds away

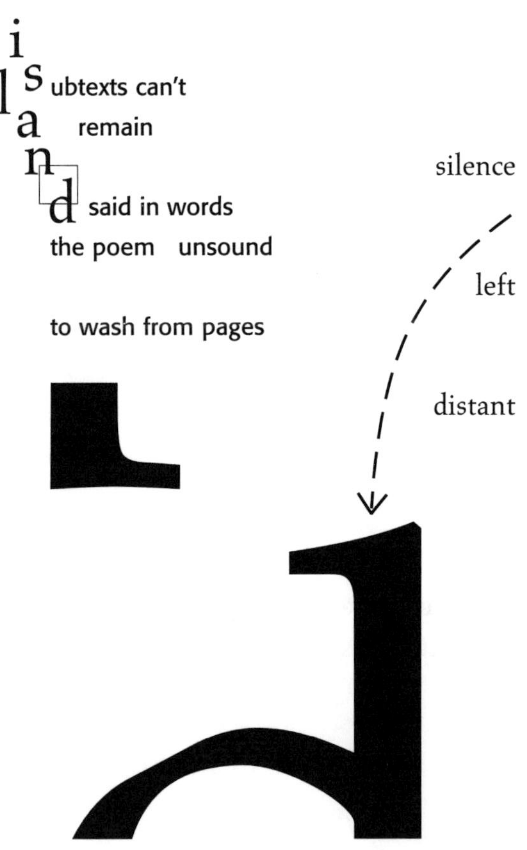
i
l s ubtexts can't
a remain
n
d said in words
the poem unsound
to wash from pages
silence
left
distant

afterberth

coded but unsignified

piercing (is) this eye
land trans
mission received
numbers spilt
spelt out

bus
t
steaming froth
photograph taken
two days after
taken
two days before
the bones picked
clean as a shadow
rising like a web
into silence taken
by breaking words
melting in the mouth like salmon

GAS FOOD

the journey is not mythic

shadowing thoughts
existing in that grey
of spoken   conception constant
                              past forming
token gift   the same need
sub
    life on asphalt
ordination   concrete blame
                                            internal compulsion
                                            fleshing out

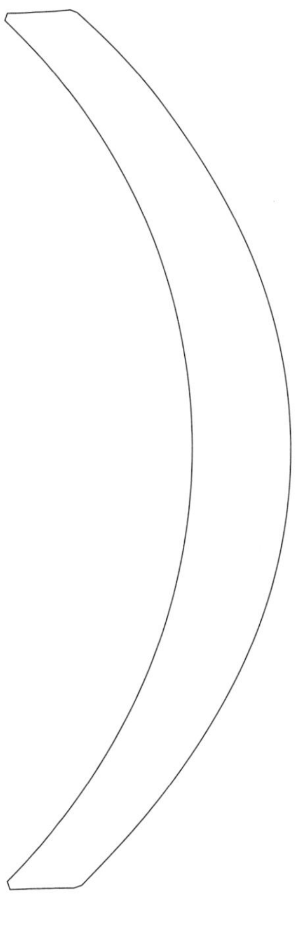

the writing becomes
a parable
comparable
to denial

a moving van
mistaken
for an ambulance

ive got the oar
ive got the oa
ive got the o
ive got the
ive got th
ive got t
ive got
ive go
ive g
ive
iv
i

continuum

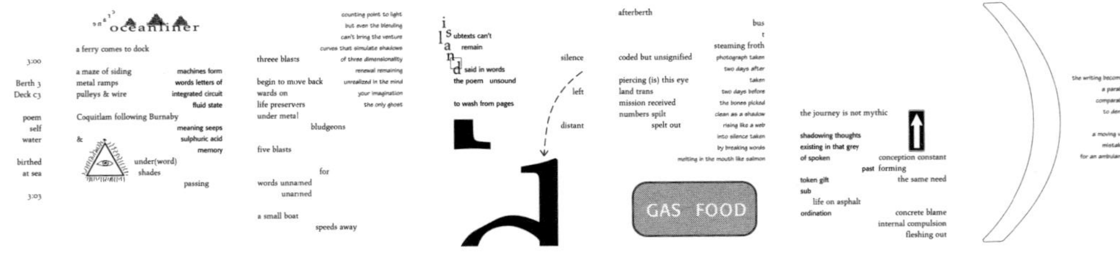

oceanliner
3:00
a ferry comes to dock
a maze of siding
metal ramps
pulleys & wire
machines form
words letters of
integrated circuit
fluid state
Berth 3
Deck c3
poem
self
water
Coquitlam following Burnaby
meaning seeps
sulphuric acid
memory
&
under(word)
shades
passing
birthed
at sea
3:03
counting point to light
but even the blending
can't bring the venture
curves that simulate shadows
of three dimensionality
renewal remaining
unrealized in the mind
your imagination
the only ghost
threee blasts
begin to move back
wards on
life preservers
under metal
bludgeons
five blasts
for
words unnamed
unarmed
a small boat
speeds away
i
s
l
a
n
d
ubtexts can't
remain
said in words
the poem unsound
to wash from pages
silence
left
distant
afterberth
bus
t
steaming froth
coded but unsignified
photograph taken
two days after
taken
piercing (is) this eye
land trans
mission received
numbers spilt
spelt out
two days before
the bones picked
clean as a shadow
rising like a web
into silence taken
by breaking words
melting in the mouth like salmon
GAS FOOD
the journey is not mythic
shadowing thoughts
existing in that grey
of spoken
conception constant
past forming
the same need
token gift
sub
life on asphalt
ordination
concrete blame
internal compulsion
fleshing out
the writing becomes
a parable
comparable
to denial
a moving van
mistaken
for an ambulance

acknowledgements

these collections have evolved slowly over the last decade, to the point where this print edition has become a companion to the electronic edition found at www.chbooks.com.

these volumes would not have been possible without the unwavering support of Anita MacFarlane, Dom Lopes, Kristen Lopes and Sara Stainton. thanks also to Daniel f. Bradley, jwcurry, brian david johnson, Dom Lopes, David UU, Darren Wershler-Henry and Alana Wilcox for support and insights over the years.

many of these pieces have been previously published, in various forms & states of completeness. thanks to the editors and publishers of: *Courier* (housepress), Curvd H&z, dbqp (USA), *fillingStation,* fingerprinting inkoperated, HUNGry zipper, *Industrial Sabotage, Ink Magazine, The Last Word* (Insomniac Press), *Lost and Found Times* (USA), *Mail Art Show/Visual Poetry* (Republic of Georgia), MindWare/Berkeley Horse, *The Mouth* (Italy), Nietzsche's Brolly, *Offerta Speciale* (Italy), *Open Letter, Oversion,* Pangen Subway Ritual, *Push Machinery, Queen Street Quarterly,* Room 302 Books, *Score* (USA), *Shit Diary, SinOverTan, The Toronto Review, Torque,* Utopic Furnace Press, *West Coast Line.*

Printed and bound in Canada at Coach House Printing on bpNichol Lane, 2000

Design by damian lopes, Bitwalla Design
Set in Formata

To read the online version of these volumes and other titles from Coach House Books, or to order any of our books, visit our website at www.chbooks.com

To add your name to our email list, write to mail@chbooks.com

Coach House Books
401 Huron Street on bpNichol Lane
Toronto ON M5S 2G5

1 800 367-6360

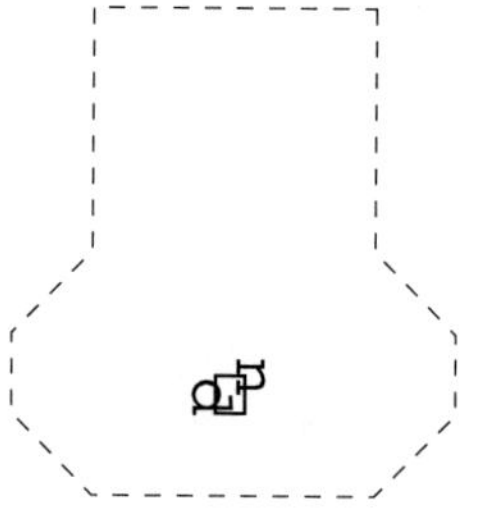

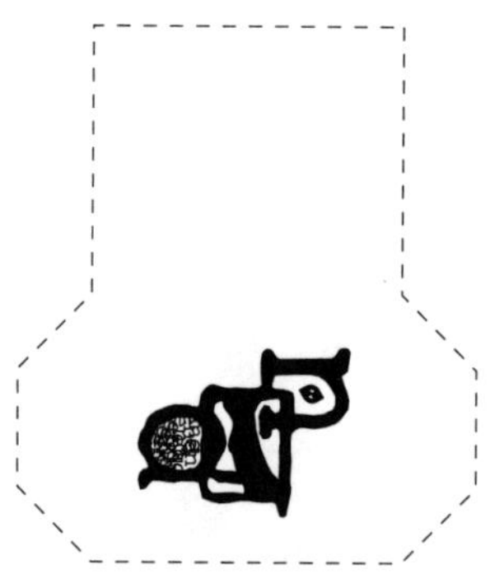

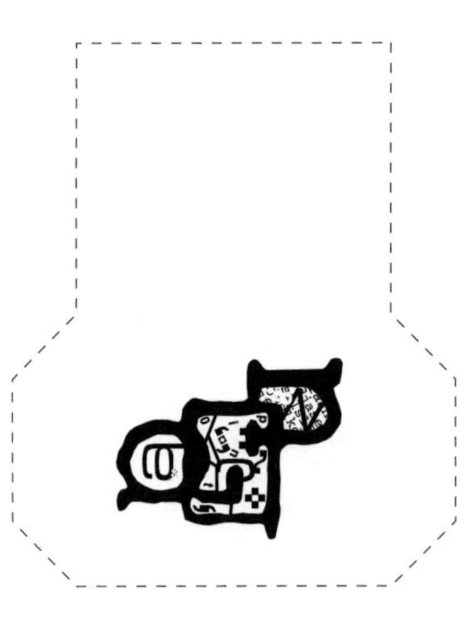

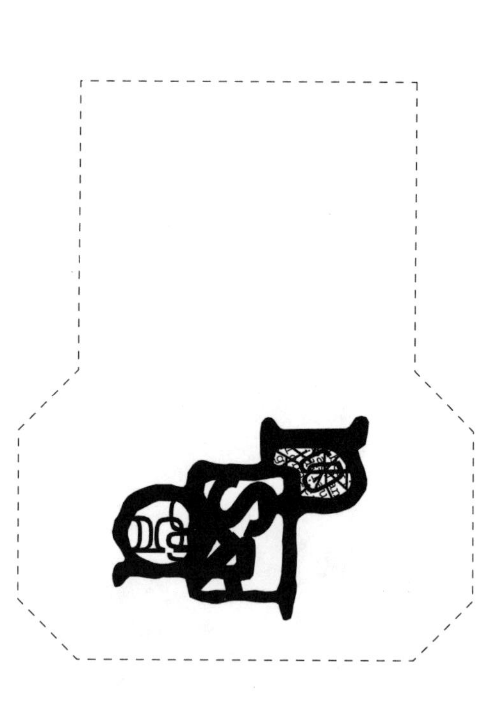

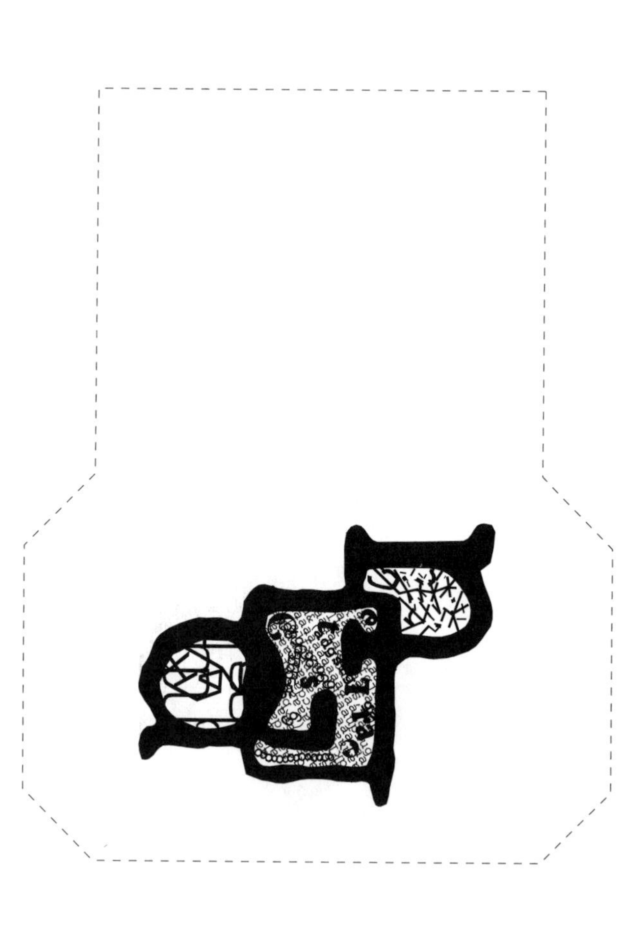

introspection instructions

- cut each page from the book
- trim each image along the dotted line
- fold each page in half, so the printed image is on the front
- fold the top and bottom flaps, and glue
- place each 'envelope' into the next larger 'envelope'

introspection

silent subtext 7 creation

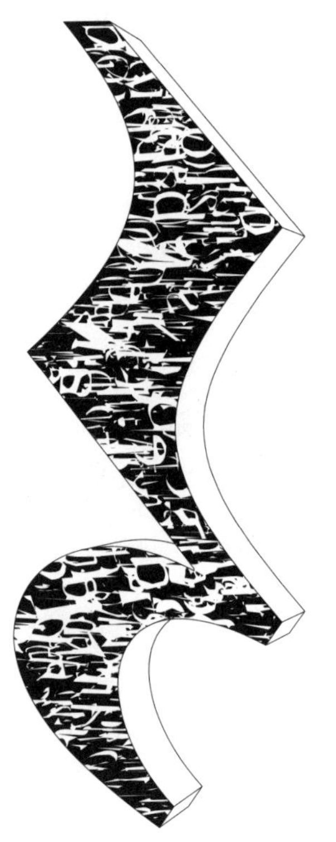

beginner's guide: enjambment

for Darren

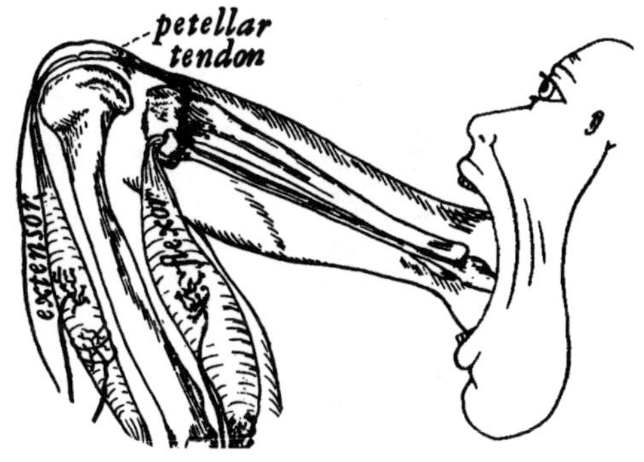

image formation of nonself

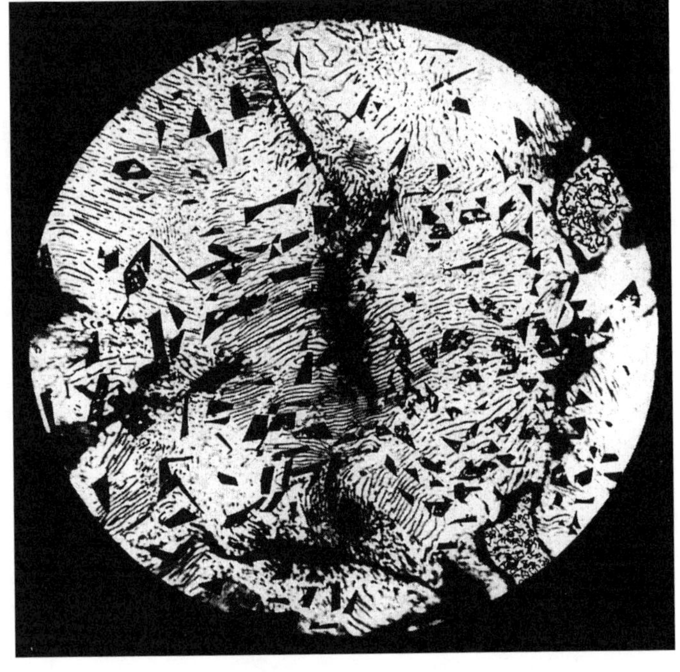

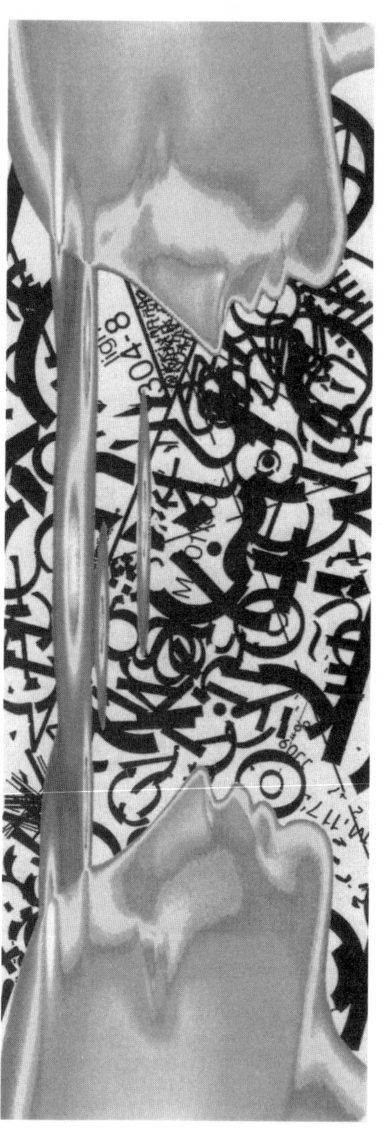

closed caption

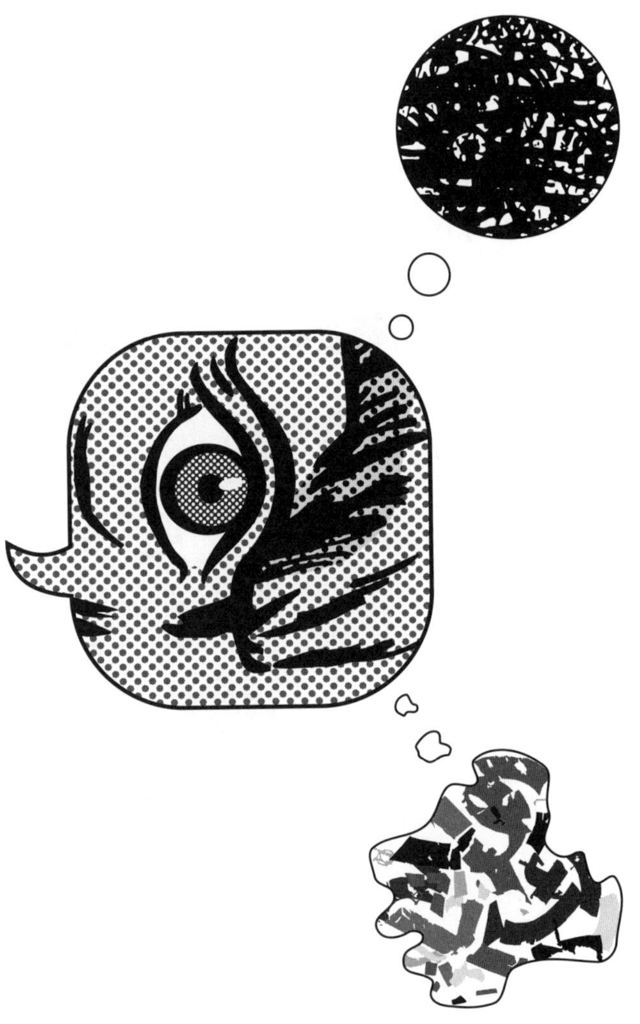

anxiety of influence

a review of Darren Wershler-Henry's **Nicholodeon**

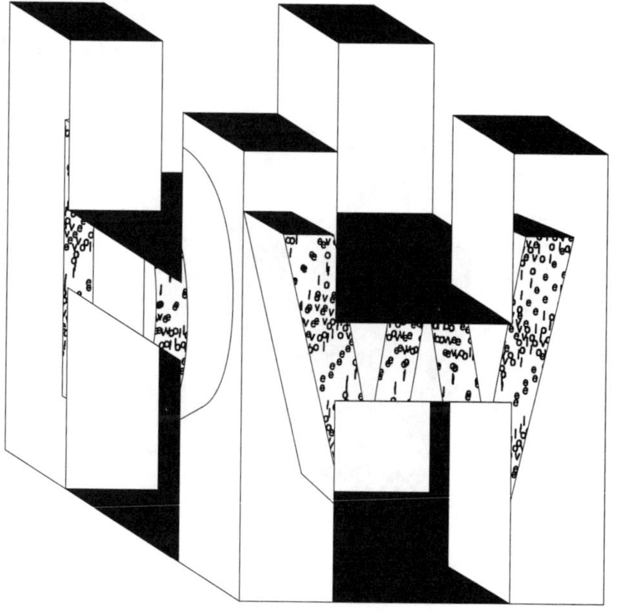

a letter to the italians

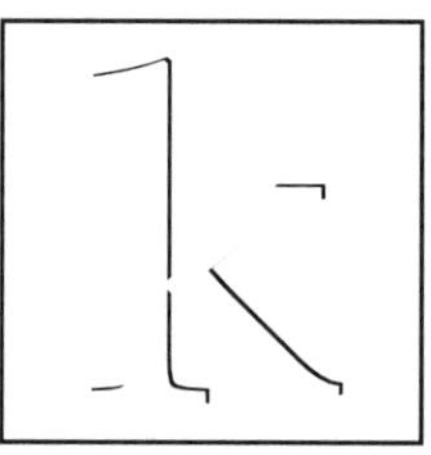

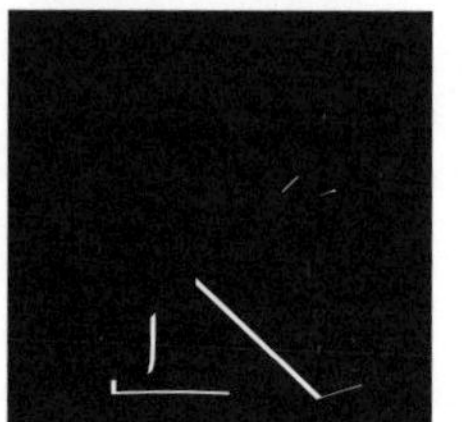

Daniel f Bradley

dreamt 1996

the mortician's waltz
la valse de l'entrepreneur de pompes funèbres
el vals del empresario de pompas fúnebres

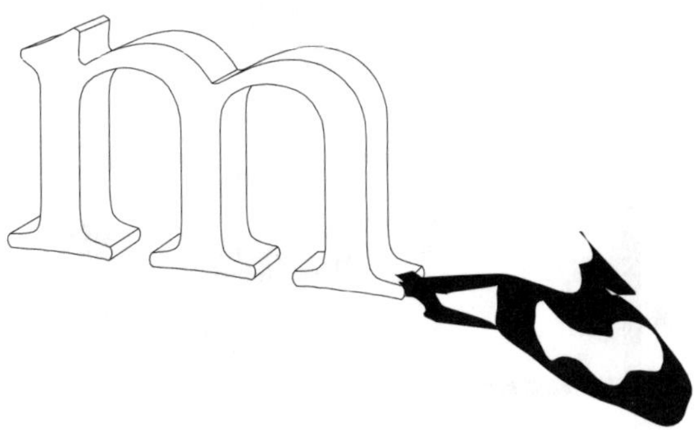
m

for m

dn

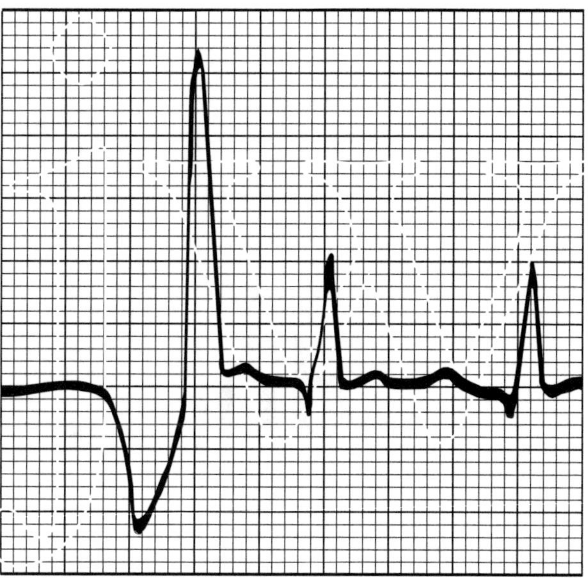

25

the sound of e

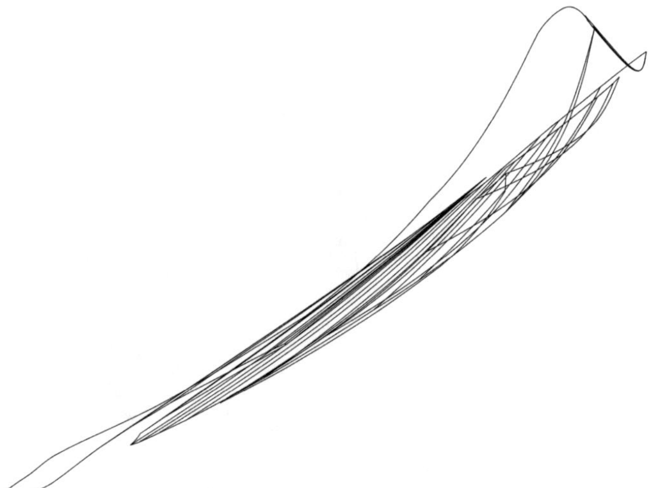

bpNichol, an untitled sound poem

dreamt 1991

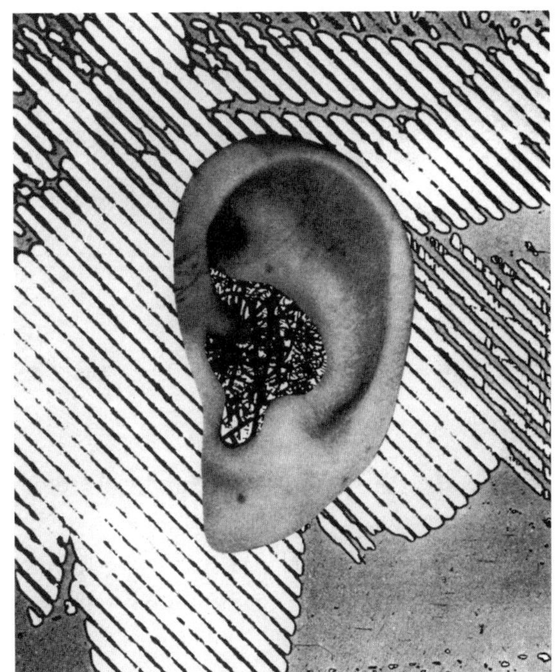

21

da

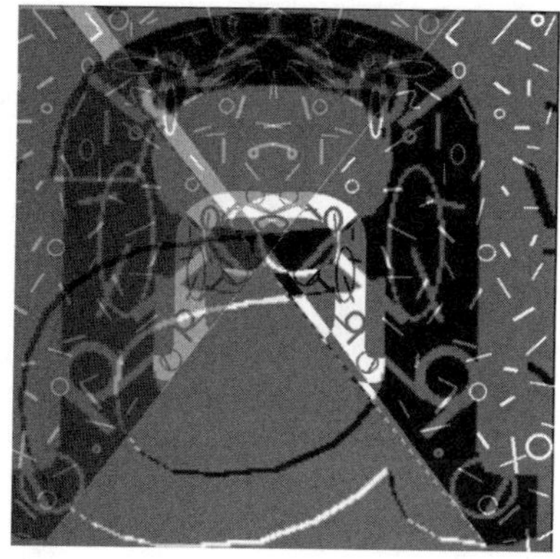

the dream of a continued

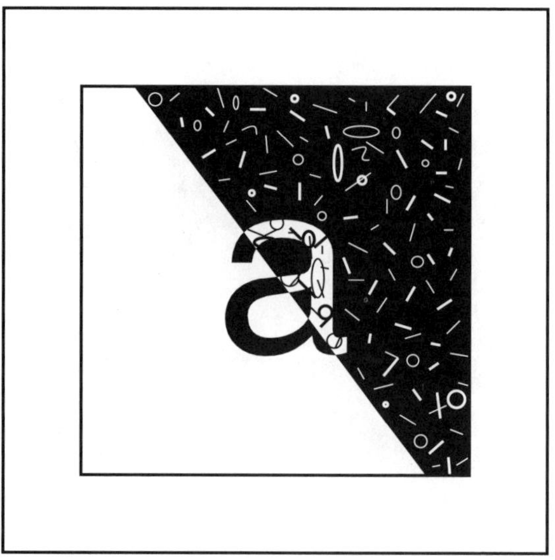

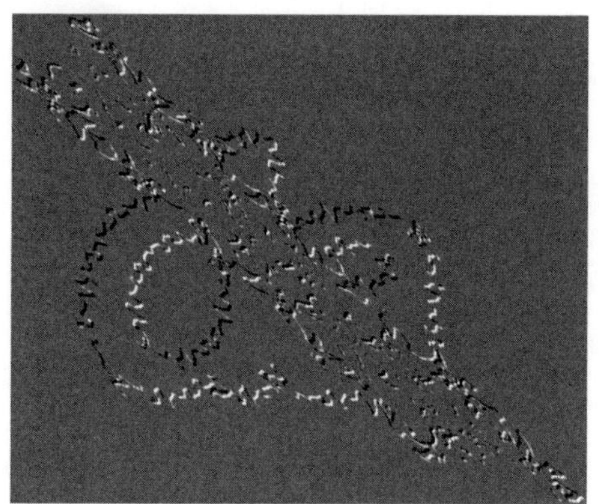

da

a comment on process

silent subtext 3 yielding seed

12

jwcurry

dreamt 1991

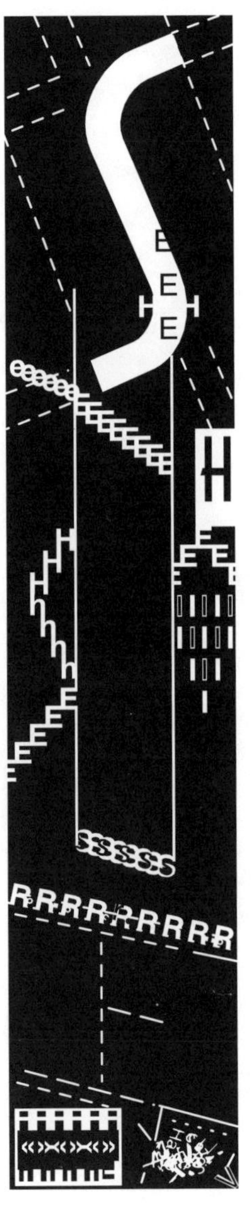

10

David UU, circa 1968

dreamt 1990

silent subtext 1 daybreak

introduction

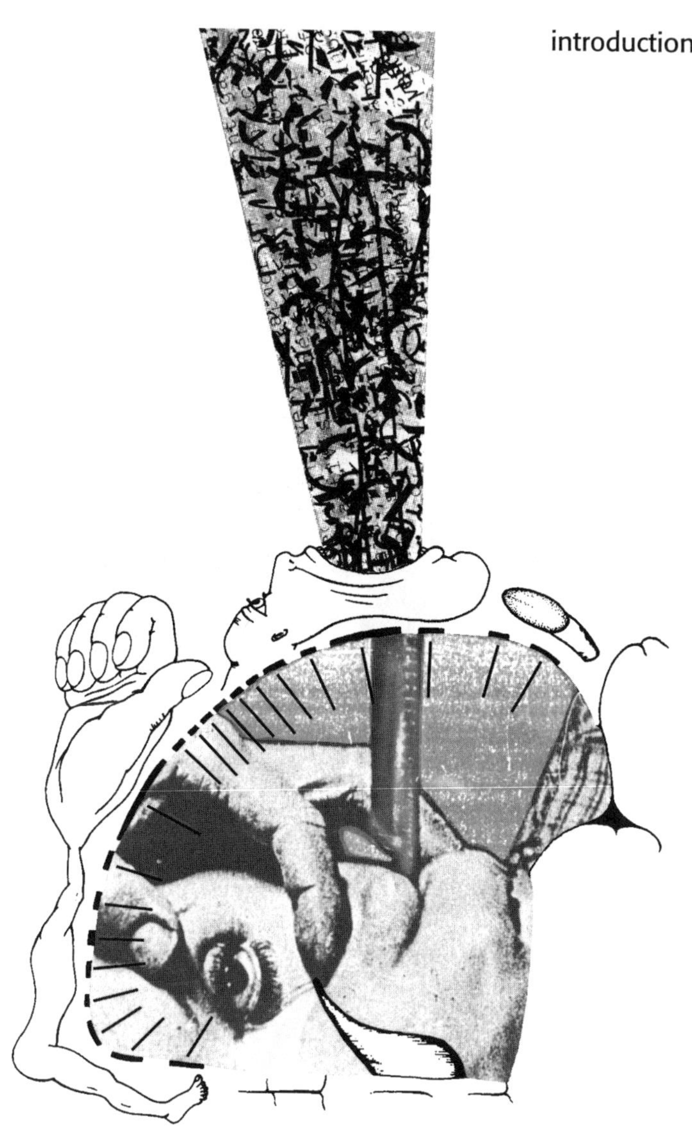

in memory of David UU

first edition

Published with the assistance of the Canada Council for the Arts and the Ontario Arts Council.

CANADIAN CATALOGUING IN PUBLICATION DATA

Lopes, Damian
Sensory deprivation

Poems.
ISBN 1-55245-052-x (boxed)
ISBN 1-55245-020-1 (pbk)

I. Title

PS8573.O637S46 2000 C811'.54 C99-930125-X
PR9199.3.L66S46 2000

dream poetics

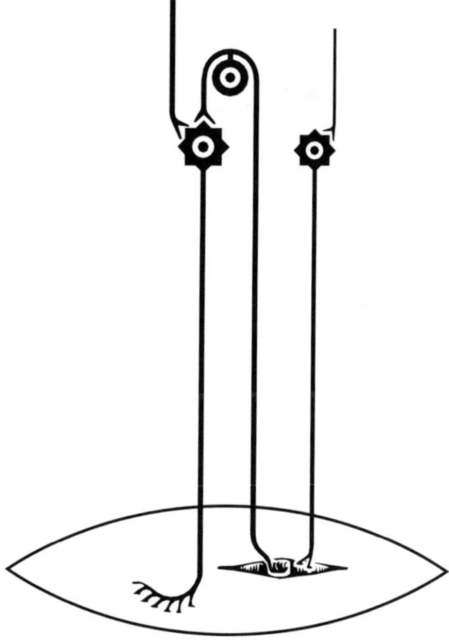

Coach House Books

dream poetics